Goddess Lakshmi
WEALTH
JOURNAL

*Make 108 Wishes for Prosperity,
Peace, and Good Fortune*

LAURIE SUE BROCKWAY

Goddess Lakshmi Wealth Journal Copyright © 2022 by Laurie Sue Brockway.

Publisher: Goddess Communications, LLC
Lakshmi cover and interior design: Qamber Designs and Media
Proofreading: by Rev. Dr. Victor Fuhrman.
Photos: Licensed from DespositPhotos.com and Shutterstock.com

Every effort has been made to ensure the accuracy of this book. The information shared in these pages is used in the spirit of educational purposes. It contains religious, cultural, and spiritual sources from a wide variety of sources for the purpose of informing and inspiring readers. Many of the classic Lakshmi poems, prayers, songs, and salutations have been used so widely that they are part of the culture, but we tried to identify the author or creator wherever possible. Classic chants about the Goddess are often evoked in goddess-honoring rituals and spiritual gatherings, and they are shared in that spirit.

Apologies to Goddess Lakshmi in advance for any errors in spelling of Sanskrit words or terms, or any error in presenting her information, prayers, or rituals.

ISBN: 978-1-941630-18-1

Photo Credits

Cover image of Lakshmi: Malgorzata_Kistryn / Shutterstock.com
Coloring image and icon of Laksmi: Natali9ka /Shutterstock.com
Pot of Gold: Dayakar Soma / Shutterstock.com
Lakshmi with pen and notebook: stockimagefactory.com / Depositphotos.com
Final Prayer Lakshmi: Watman / Depositphotos.com
Border: Alex Sunset / Shutterstock.com
Falling Coins: HobbitArt / Shutterstock.com
Final page Lakshmi: masterstrokes / Shutterstock.com
Stack of coins: New creative ideas / Shutterstock.com

Table of Contents

Increase Your Income with Lakshmi

Welcome

YEARS AGO, DURING A CHALLENGING time in my life life, I had a vision of beautiful Indian woman. She wore a green sari and had four arms, and a distinct Indian accent, but I did not know who she was at the time. I would eventually come to know and embrace her as the Goddess Lakshmi. In that brief moment, when she appeared to me in my time of need, she said, "Build a shrine to me." Acting on her message, I spent years researching everything there is to know about this popular goddess. It changed my life in extraordinary ways and set me on a path of love, success, and happiness.

Lakshmi is the Hindu Goddess of Fortune born of Indian heritage and worshipped by Hindu people in all corners of the globe. Lakshmi is also worshipped world-wide by adoring devotees and fans who take an interfaith or Goddess-based approach to religion and spirituality. Lakshmi is a Universal Goddess who can be called upon by anyone of any faith who chooses a spiritual focus for bringing more good fortune into their lives.

Over the years, I have written several books meant to help people attain Lakshmi's blessings. I have also written books to help people learn many aspects of Goddess spirituality and history. But I always come back to work with Lakshmi. She has become my spiritual mother.

In 1998 I went through a deeply challenging time. I was trying to take care of my young son with serious health issues as a single mother and I was trying to find my footing in life after a number or devastating losses. I left my career as a magazine editor to become a minister, in hopes of creating a better life for us. But I was financially strapped, and I did not have the emotional and spiritual resources (or life partner) I have today. I was stressed!

I went to see a Vedic Astrologer to ask for guidance on caring for my son, finding my soulmate, and bringing more prosperity, peace, and good fortune into my life in my work with Lakshmi.

"Honoring Lakshmi will bring you luck," he said, handing me a piece of somewhat faded paper. "But this will also help." It was called *Sri Mahalakshmi-Ashtakam Stotram,* and it had both a prayer to the goddess and instructions on how to use it. One side was English, and the other was Sanskrit.

He suggested I follow it for thirty days. I would chant it while looking at an image of Lakshmi. Things in my life began to change and my finances improved quickly. I wasn't making a million dollars, but I got a book project that helped me finish seminary school and that allowed my son and I to thrive after a period of lack and fear. I also met my soulmate.

During the pandemic I started to use the prayer again and decided to put it in a format that may help others, hence, I created the *Goddess Lakshmi Wealth Journal.* I don't recall the astrologer's name anymore, but he told me the prayer was for sharing so I share it here. You do not have to hail from the Hindu tradition to use their prayer, but you must use it with sincerity and reverence to Goddess Lakshmi.

I added some ideas for implementing the prayer in conjunction with making wishes! I hope this makes it fun, and also, that it helps you find more prosperity, peace, and good fortune in life.

Blessings,
Rev. Laurie Sue

Get to Know Lakshmi

I invoke Sri (Lakshmi), the blissful goddess, who is sweet-smiling, who lives in a hall of gold, who is full of compassion and drenched with it from the heart, who is resplendent at the seat of the lotus, is lotus-hued, and who bestows all pleasures to her devotees.
—SRI SUKTA, FROM THE RIG VEDA

LAKSHMI IS THE HINDU GODDESS of good fortune and beauty. She is actively worshipped around the globe by millions of Hindus and interfaith practitioners of goddess spirituality, and personifies abundance, prosperity, and wealth. It is said that three millennia ago, Lakshmi was born, fully grown, on a pink lotus that rose from the milky sea. She was immediately bedecked, bejeweled, and worshipped by the gods and sages. They prayed that she would come to their abodes, and to their worlds, because they believed that where Lakshmi is, one finds riches and fulfillment. "Believers" of all faiths trust that praying to the goddess of fortune brings all things good to life. Her eternal consort is Lord Vishnu, known as the Preserver, and her cohort is Ganesh, the elephant-headed Lord of Obstacles. Lakshmi, like many Hindu deities, is often pictured as a beautiful Indian woman with big dark eyes and four arms. Most Hindu shopkeepers and businesspeople keep her image in their place of business because they believe she brings them luck. With a sari-clad form that is very feminine and full, she sits or stands on her lotus throne. She usually holds two lotuses in her two hands at the back. Her front arms offer blessings and what are known as "boons" or favors from the gods. Her ability to enhance good fortune is symbolized by the gold coins that you see pouring from her hands back into the ocean of life.

Embrace Lakshmi Consciousness

WE ALL NEED THE FINANCIAL wherewithal to live comfortable lives. Great riches are not just found in money but having cash on hand helps and it also adds to our peace of mind.

We may think that one of our biggest problems around money is *not having enough of it*. But the real issues often run deeper. We may not feel worthy. We may not feel capable of earning or managing it. We may tend to zone out when it comes to money and feel afraid of attending to and nurturing our financial lives. Money is one of those highly charged issues. How does a person evolve from someone who lives paycheck to paycheck to someone who lives their dreams? It requires taking full financial responsibility. It's a growth process, to make the transition from someone who still can't balance a checkbook—all those quick debit card withdrawals make it so tricky—to someone who doesn't really *have to* balance it meticulously because there is always more than enough in the account. To create a situation of constant cash flow in our lives, we have to face our financial demons and adopt a prosperity consciousness. Or, in this case, let's call it "Lakshmi Consciousness."

Lakshmi can help increase your income in magical ways and she can bring financial stability even in the most challenging times. She can cut through fears and worries and help you manifest a better life. She grants and delivers good fortune in the material and spiritual realms.

Ask the Goddess of Good Fortune for Help

THIS JOURNAL HAS 108 DESIGNATED pages to fill with your wishes, hopes, dreams, and goals.

This number is significant to the Goddess Lakshmi, as her name is often chanted 108 times in worship service, and people use mala beads with 108 beads to pray to her. Use this book to tell Lakshmi your needs and let her help you activate good fortune in your life.

At the end of each page, write, "Thank you, Lakshmi."

Lakshmi's providence over prosperity, love, and happiness inspires us to claim our divine rights to riches and joy. Lakshmi helps you see your own potential and offers the spiritual stamina to meet it. As you open to her gifts, she will help you open you to your gifts.

Try this Daily Lakshmi Writing Ritual

- Sit down in a quiet place for 15 minutes each morning.
- Gaze at Lakshmi's beautiful image on the front cover to help you focus.
- Gaze at the mystical Sri Yantra on the back cover to connect to the cosmos and relax.
- Write what is in your heart and ask the Goddess for Her help.
- Honor Her by reciting the ancient traditional prayer: *Sri Mahalakshmi-Ashtakam Stotram*
- Use a Lakshmi Affirmation: "My life is rich in so many ways."

Feel free to replace or add in different images, prayers, blessings, and petitions.

Directions for *Sri Mahalakshmi-Ashtakam Stotram*

THIS STOTRAM, IN MANY WAYS, tells her whole mythology, reveals her auspicious symbols, explains her mission, acknowledges her supreme power, and gives tips on how to liberate oneself from darkness and attain wealth. It sometimes is accompanied by these instructions:

- This hymn to the Great Goddess of Wealth, if read with devotion, will bestow all success, will grant all worldly possessions.
- If read once a day, great sins will be destroyed.
- If always read twice a day, wealth and prosperity will ensue.
- If always read three times a day, the great enemy (ego) will be destroyed. Mahalakshmi will ever be pleased with that auspicious one.

Read the *Sri Mahalakshmi-Ashtakam Stotram*

Salutations to you, Mahamaya, abode of fortune, worshipped by gods, wielder of conch and mace, Mahalakshmi, obeisance to you.

Salutations, O rider of Garuda, terror of the demon Kola, remover of sins, beloved Goddess, Mahalakshmi, obeisance to you.

Knower of all, giver of all boons, a terror to the wicked, remover of all sorrows, beloved Goddess, Mahalakshmi, obeisance to you.

Bestower of intelligence and success, Oh Goddess, bestower of worldly enjoyment and liberation, with the mantra always as your form, Goddess Mahalakshmi, obeisance to you.

Without beginning or end, Oh Goddess, primordial energy, great Mistress born of yoga, Mahalakshmi, obeisance to you.

In the form of the gross and the subtle bodies, Rudra's Shakti, source of all, remover of great sins, beloved goddess, Mahalakshmi, obeisance to you.

Seated on a lotus, Oh Goddess, true self of the supreme Brahman, Oh Supreme Mistress, Universal Mother, Mahalakshmi, obeisance to you.

Clad in white apparel, Oh Goddess, bedecked with a variety of jewels, supporter of the universe, Universal Mother, Mahalakshmi, obeisance to you.

—Traditional 8 Verse Prayer

Just Ask Lakshmi

EVERY DAY IS ANOTHER CHANCE to honor the Goddess of Good Fortune and ask her to grant you material and spiritual wealth.

Lakshmi is a great Mother Goddess who wants to bring joy to her children. Before you ask that a wish be granted, you can release your problems and your fears to her for Divine healing.

Then it is most important that you focus on what you need and want to create and begin to imagine what life would be like if your wishes come true.

Each day you petition Lakshmi is another day you raise your energy and your faith in the abundance of the universe.

For the purpose of sending a clear intention to the Goddess, phrase each request with gratitude, as if it has already occurred.

You don't have to wait 108 days to see results.

You can also choose to make more than one wish a day. For example, you can just make more wishes on days when you have special needs, or you can consciously divide the wishes into organized segments, such as four wishes a day for 27 days, or nine wishes a day over the course of twelve days.

Just keep on working with the journal until the 108th wish page to help change your prosperity consciousness and to stay committed to drawing goodness into your life.

Imbue this Image with Your Gratitude

Start by coloring your gratitude into this image of Lakshmi. With each color you add, thank her in advance for coming into your life and helping you make your dreams come true.

Write Your 108 Wishes on the Pages That Follow

Wish #1

Wish #2

Wish #3

Wish #4

Wish #5

Wish #6

Wish #7

Wish #8

Wish #9

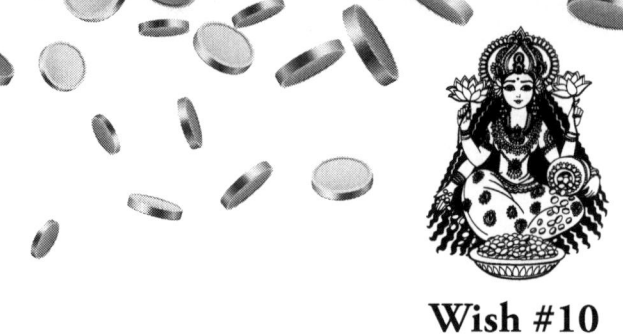

Wish #10

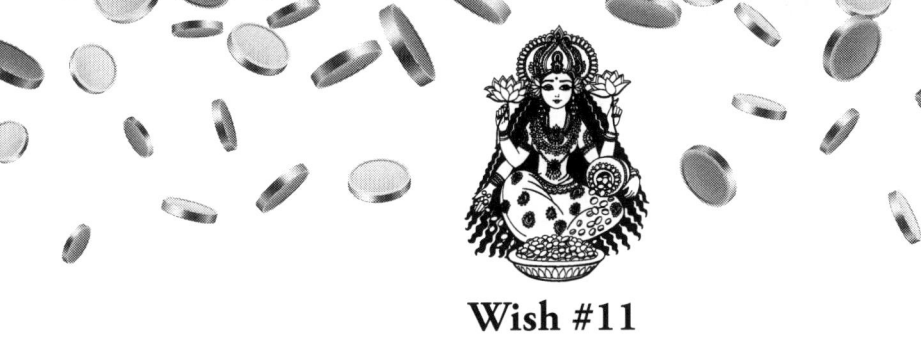

Wish #11

Wish #12

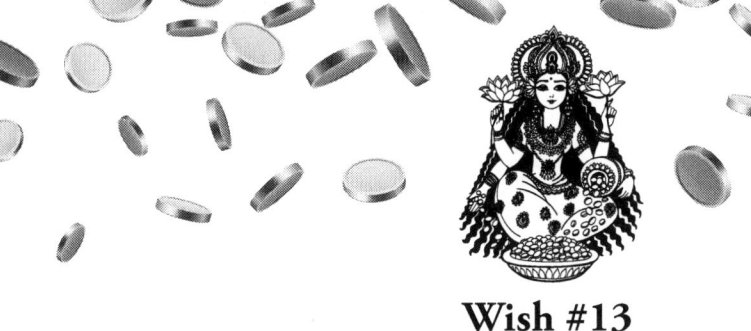

Wish #13

Wish #14

Wish #15

Wish #16

Wish #17

Wish #18

Wish #19

Wish #20

Wish #21

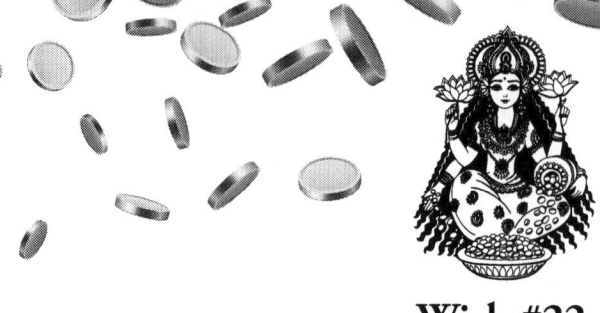

Wish #22

Wish #23

Wish #24

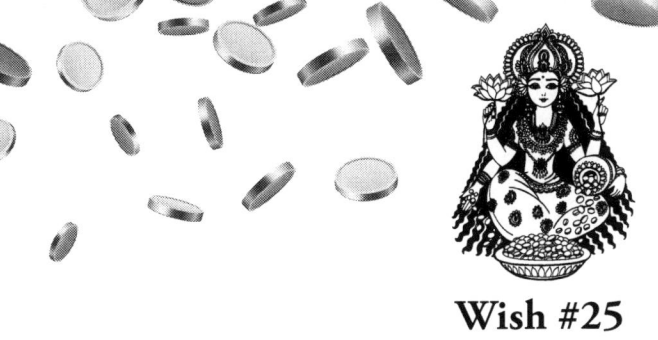

Wish #25

Wish #26

Wish #27

Wish #28

Wish #29

Wish #30

Wish #31

Wish #32

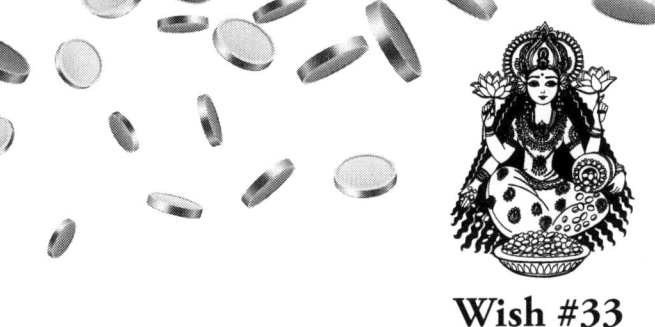

Wish #33

Wish #34

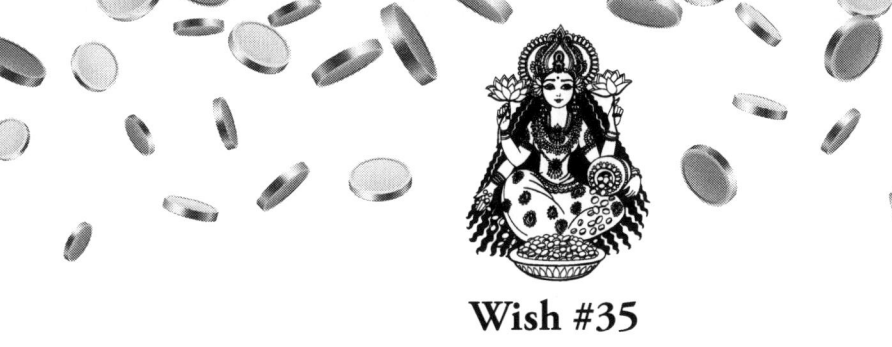

Wish #35

Wish #36

Wish #37

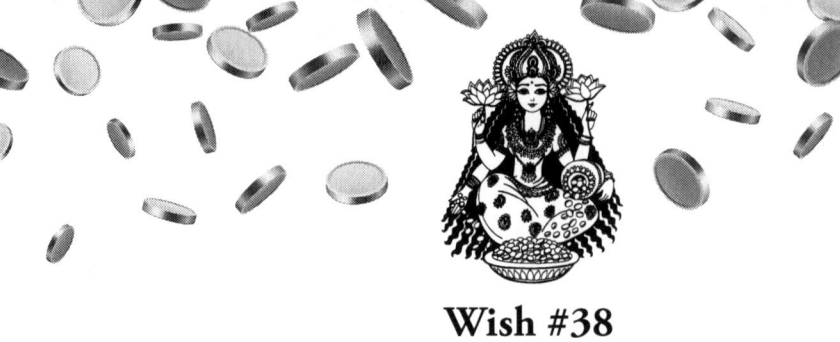

Wish #38

Wish #39

Wish #40

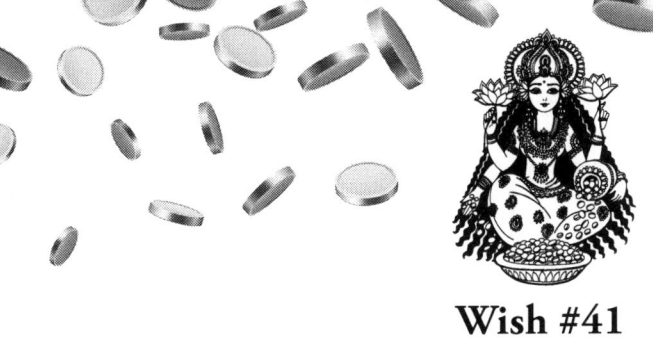

Wish #41

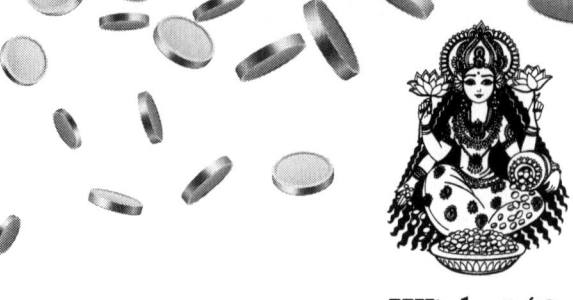

Wish #42

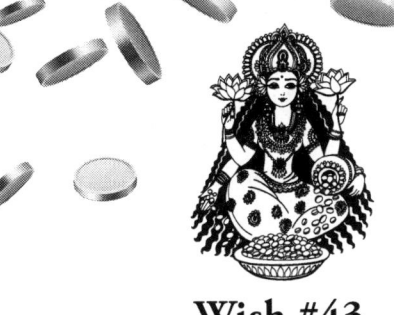

Wish #43

Wish #44

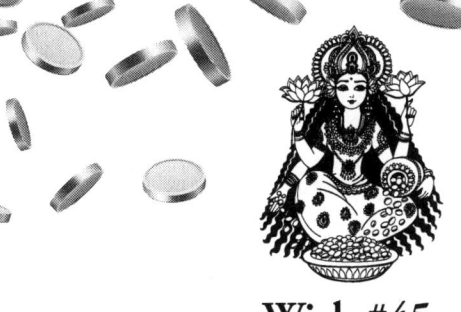

Wish #45

Wish #46

Wish #47

Wish #48

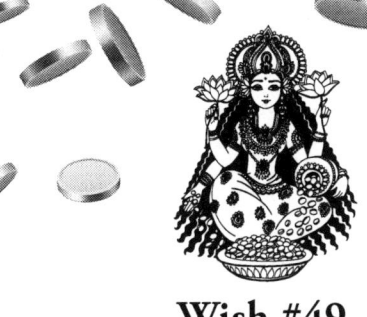

Wish #49

Wish #50

Wish #51

Wish #52

Wish #53

Wish #54

Wish #55

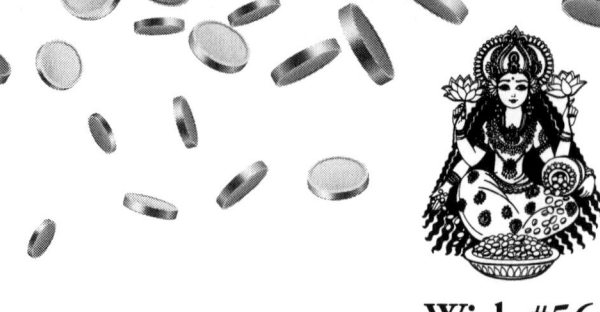

Wish #56

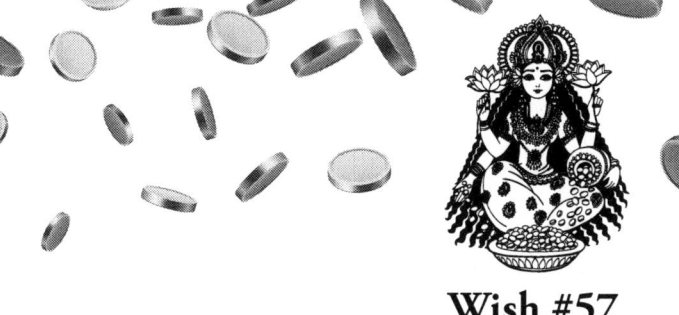

Wish #57

Wish #58

Wish #59

Wish #60

Wish #61

Wish #62

Wish #63

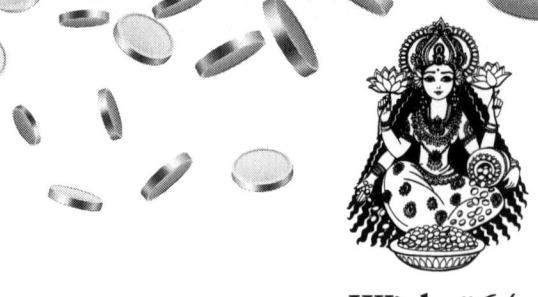

Wish #64

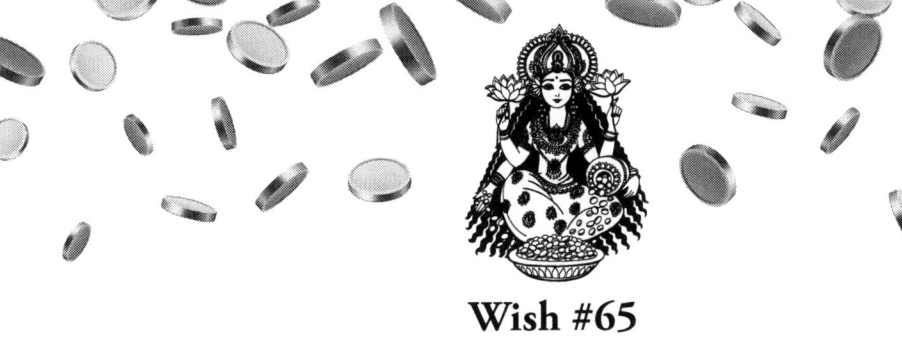

Wish #65

Wish #66

Wish #67

Wish #68

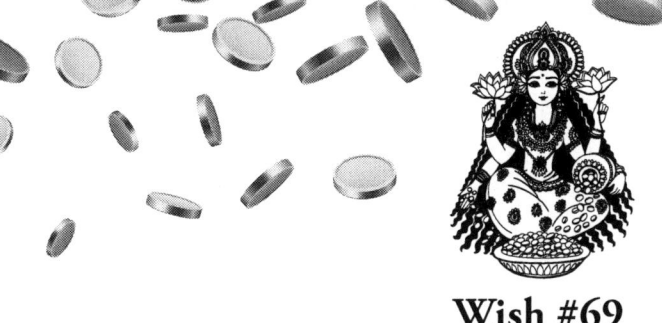

Wish #69

Wish #70

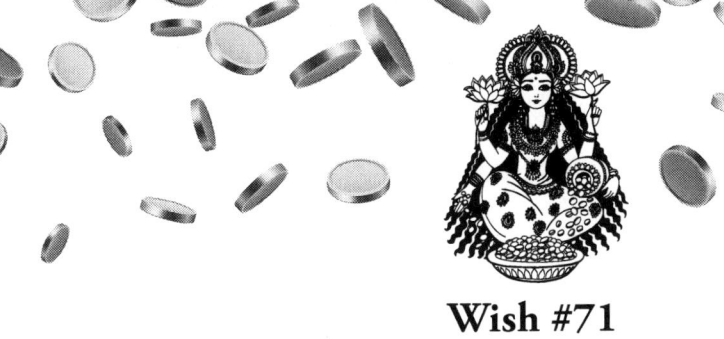

Wish #71

Wish #72

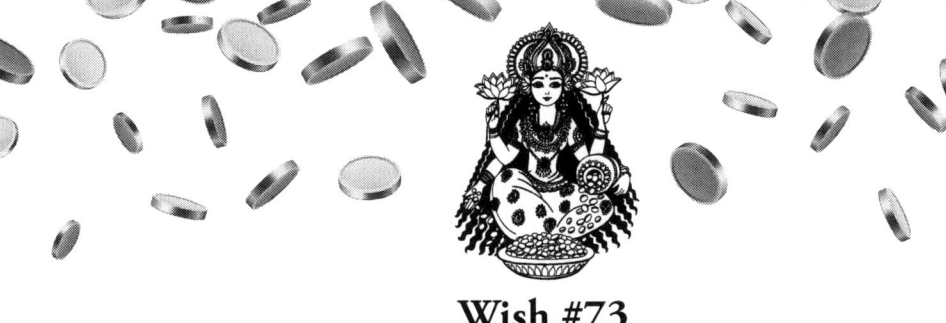

Wish #73

Wish #74

Wish #75

Wish #76

Wish #77

Wish #78

Wish #79

Wish #80

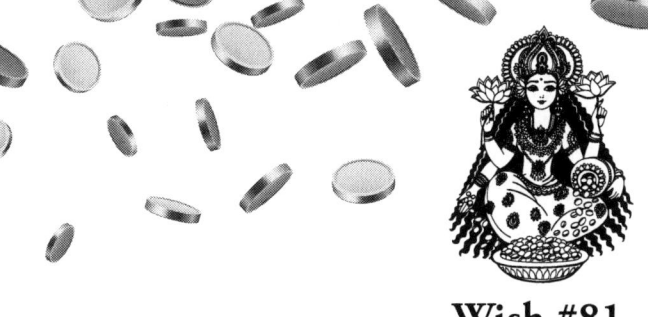

Wish #81

Wish #82

Wish #83

Wish #84

Wish #85

Wish #86

Wish #87

Wish #88

Wish #89

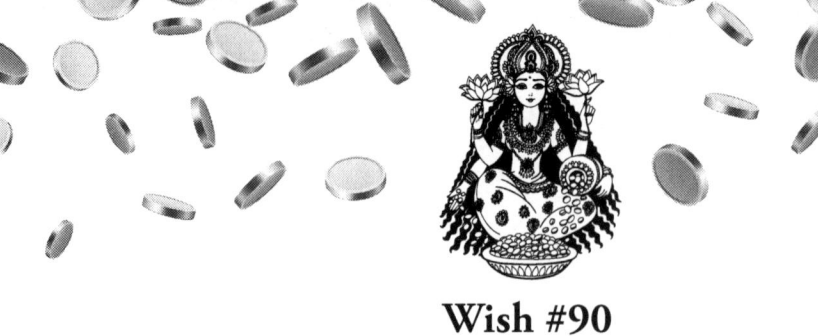

Wish #90

Wish #91

Wish #92

Wish #93

Wish #94

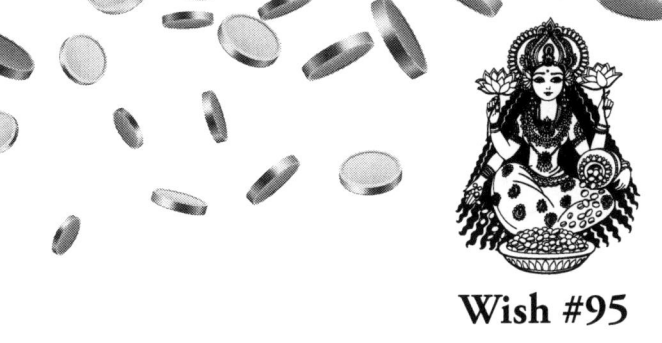

Wish #95

Wish #96

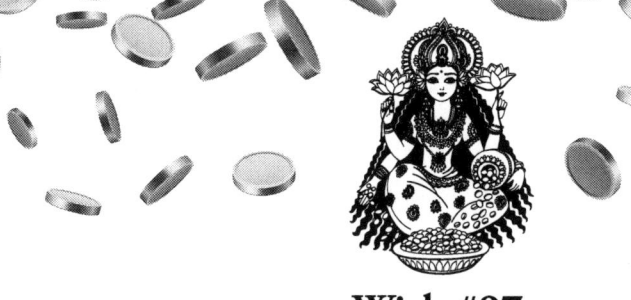

Wish #97

Wish #98

Wish #99

Wish #100

Wish #101

Wish #102

Wish #103

Wish #104

Wish #105

Wish #106

Wish #107

Wish #108

NOTES

Bonus Feature

Make a Symbolic Gesture Toward Prosperity: Start a Lakshmi Prosperity Bank

LAKSHMI IS HONORED WHEN YOU place her picture or icon in your home. Get a small statue or postcard of Lakshmi (widely available online) and build a small "bank" in honor of the goddess of fortune. Your Lakshmi bank will be a mini shrine, a place where you will commune with the goddess, and, ideally, the place where you will organize and honor your financial life in her presence.

CHOOSE A PLACE FOR YOUR BANK-SHRINE. It should be positioned so that you can see it every day, and have an area designated for paying bills and dealing with finances. No matter where you place it, it should be easily accessible to you. If you must stash it out of sight, place it in a southeast closet or room and visit her frequently.

GET A CLEAR GLASS VASE. This will be your Lakshmi bank and as you fill it with coins, you will see your prosperity grow.

PLACE LAKSHMI'S PICTURE OR ICON NEAR YOUR BANK. If you don't wish to use her picture, simply view the bank as a vital essence of Lakshmi's prosperous energy and dedicate it to her.

START YOUR BANK WITH FOUR SHINY NEW U.S. QUARTERS OR COINS FROM YOUR REGION. These represent Lakshmi's four arms; symbolically the new coins will initiate financial flow. Taking the time to quiet yourself and feel relaxed, offer the coins to the goddess as if you are giving a divine gift. People often make offerings to Lakshmi using the right hand. But you can also make offerings by prayerfully using both hands, cupped, and gently spilling the coins into the bank. As you do so, thank her *for all the good fortune that she is now pouring into your life, and for all areas of your financial life that she will empower and help you develop.*

ADD FOUR COINS DAILY FOR THIRTY DAYS. If you don't have four quarters every day, use the coins you do have. Just make sure you share your good fortune with the goddess daily. Spend a moment of sacred silence every time you drop a coin in and acknowledge the increasing finances. The sight of your money growing, and the sense that *you are growing it with your own hands* with the goddess's help, will instill you with greater confidence and inspiration.

DO ALL YOUR FINANCIAL TASKS AT THE BANK-SHRINE. As you add money to it, it adds power to your financial life, so it becomes a sacred space in which to manage all your money-related tasks. Write your checks, pay your bills, and review your credit card records in front of Lakshmi. If you don't have a checking account, start one now—and fill out the application forms in front of the bank-shrine. (You should also have a savings account!) When you're feeling brave, balance your checkbook. Get in the habit of evoking Lakshmi in all things financial.

WHEN THE BANK IS FULL, REMOVE THE MONEY AND COUNT IT. First, following the spiritual law of tithing, put 10 percent aside for a worthy cause that you would like to support. Put the rest in a savings account and dedicate it as an offering to the goddess Lakshmi.

WATCH YOUR MONEY GROW AGAIN! Have fun filling up your Lakshmi bank again (and again). At the end of each thirty-day cycle, add more money to your savings account.

Lakshmi Affirmation
"My life is rich in so many ways."

Final Blessing

Dearest Lakshmi,
Please come into my life.
Fill my home with your sacred presence.
Honor me with your protection and your prosperous ways.
Please bring your riches both spiritual and material.
Help me find fulfillment and success.
Enhance my good fortune so that I can help others.
Please pour your gold coins into my life.
Om Shrim Maha Lakshmiyei Swaha
My grateful heart fills with respect and admiration.
In advance, I thank you.

Goddess Lakshmi Wealth Journal
Bibliography and Attributions

Author's note: As a longtime fan of Lakshmi, I have studied her history and worship since 1998. Some of the ideas in *Goddess Lakshmi Wealth Journal* were drawn from my years of observing rituals in Hindu temples and my prior writings about her.

"Get to Know Lakshmi" quote: *The Holy Vedas: Rig Veda, Yajur Veda, Sama Veda, Atharva Veda* (New Delhi: B.R. Publishing, 2006). From the "Sri Sukta," Rig Veda.

Ganesh chant: Sri Swami Sivananda, cited at "Ganesha," www. dlshq. org/ religions/ganesha.htm.

Upendra Nath Dhal. 1995. *Goddess Lakshmī : Origin and Development*. Delhi: Eastern Book Linkers.

Dipavali Debroy, *Laksmi Puja* (Delhi: Hindi Pocket Books, 1996).

Dipavali Debroy, and Bibek Debroy. 2003. *The Padma Purana*. Delhi: Books For All, New Delhi.

Laurie Sue Brockway. 2020. *Lakshmi Magic*. 2nd ed. New York City: Goddess Communications, LLC.

Laurie Sue Brockway. *Lakshmi Devotional*. 1st ed. New York City: Goddess Communications, LLC.

Laurie Sue Brockway. 2008. *The Goddess Pages: A Divine Guide to Finding Love and Happiness*. Woodbury, Minn.: Llewellyn Publications.

Note about Sri Mahalakshmi-Ashtakam Stotram: I do not recall the name of the Vedic Astrologer who first gave me the prayer. A current version can be found here: http://cayelincastell.com/wp-content/uploads/2015/11/Lakshmi-Prayer.pdf

About Laurie Sue Brockway

Rev. Laurie Sue Brockway has been blessed with Goddess Lakshmi's presence and guidance for twenty-five years.

She has written extensively on goddess spirituality and history, self-esteem, emotional health, relationships, and weddings. She has published thousands of articles and more than twenty-five books, including, *Lakshmi Magic, Alakshmi, Lakshmi Devotional, The Goddess Pages, Goddess Lessons, Wedding Goddess, Your Interfaith Wedding, Your Hindu-Interfaith Ceremony, Pet Prayers and Blessings, Seshat Journal*, and *She Who Scrivens*.

Her deep interest in goddess studies began when she was a journalist specializing in women's empowerment, and it led her to become an ordained minister focused on interfaith ceremonies and women's spirituality.

For over two decades she has presided over a multicultural wedding ministry based in New York and is widely recognized as an expert on interfaith, intercultural, and highly personalized nondenominational weddings. She has officiated many Hindu-Interfaith weddings. The foundation of her ministry is to celebrate all faiths and traditions and to include all aspects of the Divine.

She received her psychology B.A. degree in Human Development from SUNY and attended graduate school for Marriage and Family Therapy. She is also a graduate of The New Seminary for Interfaith Studies, where she was ordained in 1999, and where she returned to complete advanced spiritual studies. She received her Master of Interfaith Studies (M.Is) in 2020 and Doctor of Ministry (D.Min) in 2021. Her dissertation was on the Goddess Lakshmi. She is currently studying the intersection of the Divine Feminine and public history.

Other Books from Goddess Communications, LLC

LAKSHMI MAGIC

We can all use more money, great job opportunities, and goodness in life. This book tells you how to invite material and spiritual wealth on all levels. And it gives you dozens of rituals, prayers, and techniques to draw prosperity and beauty into your life with the help of Goddess Lakshmi. Lakshmi, the Hindu Goddess of Good Fortune, has been bringing good things to life for five thousand years.

In this small but powerful book, the author reveals the spiritual secrets she learned and adapted during many years of study. The writing is fun and easy to follow. You will discover:

- The mythology and meaning of Lakshmi
- How to invite her grace into your life
- Rituals and devotions to attract Lakshmi's attention
- Prayers to ask for her blessings
- Insights into traditional Hindu worship
- Ideas for inviting good fortune into your life
- Peace of mind in times of financial struggle

Lakshmi is famous and beloved for her awesome role of bringing prosperity, opportunity, and success into your life.

Create a Circle of Good Fortune in your life. Learn how to develop a relationship and spiritual practice with the beautiful Hindu Goddess of material and spiritual wealth, Lakshmi.

She is a bright light and a beautiful sacred mother who brings love, joy, prosperity, and spiritual and material wealth. She helps increase finances and improves your state of being. She has many roles and faces in the Hindu tradition and she is also a universal goddess who blesses people of all backgrounds.

This book takes you on a journey to discover many ways to honor Lakshmi as well as many ways to connect with her in deep, soulful, and magical ways. It guides you to traditional and ancient worship and shares many secrets for modern times.

When you honor Lakshmi—as a Goddess, Divine Guide, and Spiritual Support System—you can become skillful at creating good fortune and miracles. You can also help loved ones and be generous to others.

Lakshmi favors those who follow the true path of the heart and soul, and who truly want to make room for her blessings and power in their lives.

Did you know that Lakshmi, the Hindu Goddess of Fortune, has a sister named Alakshmi?

The complete opposite of her beautiful sibling, Alakshmi is considered a Goddess of Bad Fortune or Misfortune. It is generally believed that where there is trouble, poverty, misery, strife, and calamity… there's Alakshmi.

This book considers that the metaphor of Alakshmi presents an opportunity for us to take a look at the aspects of our lives that are chaotic, out-of-control, negative, and void of good fortune. Accepting and honoring Alakshmi's existence can help us accept our own inner chaos and begin to transform negativity.

In this book you will discover:

- The meaning of Alakshmi
- Why people want to get rid of her
- How she is worshipped
- The importance of embracing your inner dark twin
- Tips to release the things that clutter your mind and home
- How to inventory your life, make plans, and take action
- Rituals of good riddance to Alakshmi
- How Alakshmi can lead you to Lakshmi

Lakshmi, The Goddess of Good Fortune, is an adored divine female from the Hindu tradition who brings spiritual and material wealth. She is called upon to bless all endeavors and to help in times of financial need.

THE GODDESS PAGES

Every woman could use a bit of Goddess wisdom in her life.

Do you want to explore your personal power and claim your passions? Do you seek advancement in your career? Are you searching for love, or trying to get free of a bad romance? Do you wish you had more confidence and courage? The Divine Feminine is here to help you achieve the love, success, and happiness that you deserve.

Get ready to feel empowered: you are about to meet thirty-six of the most revered spiritual heroines from faiths and traditions around the world. Use this book to call upon each one for support, guidance, and inspiration in all areas of your life. Evoke their unique energies and strengths through rituals, meditations, gatherings, prayers, blessings, and many more fun and creative activities.

- Celebrate your true beauty with Hathor
- Unleash your dark and wild side with Lilith
- Free yourself from unhealthy relationships with Persephone
- Take aim at your career goals with Artemis
- Own and explore your sensuality with Oshun
- Find protection and healing with Tara
- Manifest spiritual and material wealth with Lakshmi

The Goddess Pages is a unique and empowering book that helps you connect with the strength and beauty of the Goddess—and experience the divine within you.

Do you yearn to connect more deeply with The Goddess? And to learn more about Goddess Spirituality in many cultures?

In this book, you will:

- Discover the wisdom, strength, and magic of the Divine Feminine
- Learn about Her history and the cultures that honor her today
- Discover ways to heal yourself and contribute to the healing of the world
- Soothe chaos and fear through sacred rituals, meditation, and prayer
- Deepen your sacred connection to yourself and the spiritual world
- See how honoring the feminine divine can activate self-esteem and self-honoring
- Connect to the Great Mother and different aspects of the Feminine Divine
- Tap into the power of the Goddess to improve your life

Just like our human mothers, the Divine Feminine can bring love, balance, and protection to our lives and to the world. She is practical and magical. We need her help. And she needs our help.

Many of us have a book inside that wants to be born. Laurie Sue Brockway - Minister, Scribal Priestess, and author of more than 25 books - is uniquely qualified to help midwife the book of your heart.

She Who Scrivens is for authors who are searching for guidance on how to blend the sacred with the practical aspects of writing and publishing. And it offers spiritual magic tricks and ancient secrets that will help you get words onto paper.

Begin your book project with special help from Seshat, the Egyptian Goddess of Writing and Scribes, who is also known as "She Who Scrivens" and "She Who Writes." Always seen with a star upon her head, she connects us to the wisdom of all that is.

Writing is a sacred act that has magical power. Embrace your own personal creative process and learn how to create a spiritual practice for writing. Discover ways to dream your book into reality and to elevate your presence as an author.

Explore the magic of writing and find your own path to publishing. The author blends ancient wisdom and practical inspiration for modern scribes.

Everyone deserves a chance to tell their story and share their wisdom with the world. Writing a book is a dream for many spiritual authors, but they may not have a way to blend the sacred with the practical to create the book of their hearts. This journal can help!

Begin your book project with special help from Seshat, the Egyptian Goddess of Writing, who is also known as "She Who Scrivens" and "She Who Writes." Always seen with a star upon her head, she connects us to the wisdom of all that is.

Seshat Journal explores the practical steps to deciding on the book you will write and ways to call in Divine Wisdom in every stage of the project to help you dream your book into reality.

GODDESS IN THE MIRROR

Some of us are born with a great sense of self, sovereignty, and self-preservation.

The rest of us need a little work in that area! And we need to learn how to see ourselves through unbiased, spiritual eyes.

This book explores a myriad of ways that those who identify as goddesses can truly step into a powerful relationship with themselves, and the Divine.

We will call on ancient Goddesses known for their mirrors, including Hathor, Venus, Oshun, and Amaterasu. And we will learn practical and metaphysical tips for leaving our inner critics behind and embracing all of who we are.

The author guides you through self-celebration ceremonies, self-honoring devotions, self-love meditations, and self-awareness exercises. She helps you create a new way of looking at yourself through the lens of love and by calling forth your inner Goddess.

The aim is to see your own reflection in a whole new light.

This long-awaited follow-up to Laurie Sue Brockway's bestselling book, *A Goddess is a Girl's Best Friend* (now available as *The Goddess Pages*), invites you to step onto a path of truly embracing your own divinity.

Goddess Communications, LLC
New York City